QUILT A KOALA

Australian Animals & Birds in Patchwork

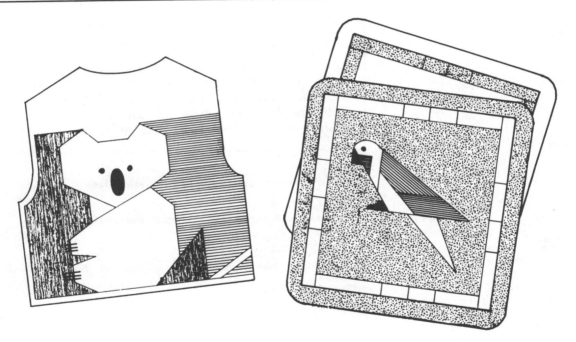

Margaret Rolfe

Illustrations by Phil Rolfe

 Sterling Publishing Co., Inc.   New York

A note from the author...

This book is dedicated to Bradley, Jordan, Curtis, Nicholas, Alison, and especially to Melinda, because they all liked my animals.

It was fun designing these animals and birds, so I hope you will gain equal pleasure sewing them. Originally I had no intention of making a book from them, but the designs kept on coming and, suddenly, there it was! The twenty designs are offered for you to use creatively. Do adapt them to your own purposes and your own quilts. We have only photographed a few of the possibilities — I hope you will discover lots more.

A book, even a small one such as this, requires a team effort from a number of people besides the author. I would like to thank Celia Pollock for her help and encouragement. I must also thank my parents, Linda and Alex Poppins, for their practical assistance. Photographer Mike Fisher and designer Zoë Gent-Murphy, both gave of their professional excellence to produce the superb colour plates. Jane Fisk and Glen Williams assisted by trying out the patchwork designs and suggesting new ideas.

I am especially grateful to Kerry Gavin, Judy Turner, Trudy Brodie, Wendy Saclier and Linda McGuire who made beautiful items to be used for photography, and who all helped and supported the book so enthusiastically.

I deeply appreciate the work of my son Phil, who contributed the wonderful animal drawings. Finally, my heartfelt gratitude is extended to my husband Barry, for whom the words "impossible" and "I can't" do not exist.

Quilt a koala, patch a possum, work a wombat ... have fun!

Margaret Rolfe

A note about the measurements

All measurements in this book are given using both metric and imperial measures. The conversions are not exact but, for purposes of clarity and practicality, care has been taken to round the imperial figures to their closest metric equivalent. The two systems are **not** interchangeable, so use only one or the other.

Library of Congress Cataloging-in-Publication Data

Rolfe, Margaret.
    Quilt a koala : Australian animals & birds in patchwork / Margaret Rolfe.
        p. cm.
    ISBN 0-8069-7264-5
    1. Patchwork—Patterns.   2. Decoration and ornament—Animal forms—Australia.   I. Title.
    TT835.R653   1990   89-78231

    746.46—dc20   CIP

Copyright text and designs © 1986 by Margaret Rolfe
Published in 1990 by Sterling Publishing Co., Inc.
387 Park Avenue South, New York, N.Y. 10016
First published in Australia in 1986 by
Wattle Books, Melbourne
Distributed in Canada by Sterling Publishing
% Canadian Manda Group, P.O. Box 920, Station U
Toronto, Ontario, Canada M8Z 5P9
Distributed in Great Britain and Europe by Cassell PLC
Artillery House, Artillery Row, London SW1P 1RT, England
Printed in Hong Kong
All rights reserved
Sterling ISBN 0-8069-7264-5 Paper

Contents

Glossary of Patchwork Terms

Appliqué   The process by which a piece of one fabric is stitched onto a background of another fabric. In this book, applique is used to add details to the animals, e.g. noses and eyes.

Bias   The direction on fabric that is at a diagonal (a 45° angle) to the grain of the fabric (see Figures 1 and 2). Fabric cut on the bias has more stretch and give than fabric cut straight on the grain, and this can sometimes be used to advantage. For instance, strips of fabric cut on the bias can be used to finish the edges of a quilt or a cushion, because the bias strips will stretch neatly around curved corners.

Block   A square of patchwork design. A block is the basic unit from which patchwork objects are constructed. In this book, each design will be called a block, e.g. the Koala block.

Grain   The direction in which the woven threads lie in a piece of fabric (see Figure 1). Both lengthwise and crosswise threads form the grain of the fabric. You will find that patchwork pieces will fit together better if the grain is kept consistent throughout the blocks. However, there are times when you might want to ignore the grain of the fabric, for a special effect. For instance, you may want to have stripes running in a particular direction, as in the Echidna. If, as a general rule, you keep the pieces of a block *on* the grain, some pieces off the grain will not matter, as long as you handle them carefully, and do not stretch them.

Piecing   The process by which pieces of fabric are sewn together to make a patchwork design. Piecing is the most basic process in patchwork, and the seams can be stitched by machine or by hand. Machine sewing is quicker, and stronger for articles that will be washed frequently. Hand-piecing is slower and not as strong, though some people prefer it because it is more portable, and can be done in company. The decision whether to work by hand or by machine is entirely personal — neither way is right nor wrong.

Quilting   The process by which three layers of material are stitched together. The patchwork top, the middle layer of batting, and a layer of backing fabric are the layers involved. Think of the three layers as a fabric 'sandwich', with the quilting going through all three layers to join them together. Quilting can be done by hand or machine.

Templates   Shapes, made from cardboard, which are the pattern pieces of the patchwork design. The pieces of fabric in patchwork must be cut out accurately so that they will fit as you sew them together. Templates ensure this accuracy.

Figure 1

The direction of the grain on a piece of fabric.

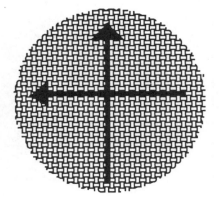

Figure 2

The direction of the bias on a piece of fabric.

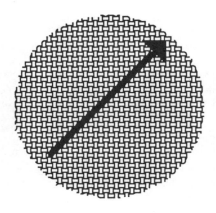

Equipment You Will Need

Sewing Machine The most important piece of equipment for patchwork. It does not have to be capable of fancy stitches; just straight stitching. For piecing (the sewing together of the patches of fabric), set your machine on a fairly short stitch length — but not so short that it is impossible to unpick should you make a mistake! The ideal stitch length will be about the number two setting on most machines. For machine quilting, it is helpful to have a machine with either dual feed built in, or a dual feed attachment, which helps the three layers of the quilt move through the machine smoothly without one of the layers moving ahead of, or behind, the others.

Quilting hoop A hoop is used to hold the three layers of the quilt sandwich as you stitch them together in the quilting process. Without a hoop the layers could shift, creating ugly puckering and bunching. A hoop consists of two wooden rings, one of which fits inside the other. The inner hoop is laid down, the quilt put smoothly across it, then the outer hoop is pressed down on top. A hoop about 35 cm-40 cm (14"-16") in diameter is a good size for the patchwork in this book, although larger hoops can be used.

Scissors Sharp dressmaking scissors are essential for patchwork, since you will be cutting out lots of pieces of fabric. Use a different pair of scissors for cutting out the cardboard templates, and a small, sharp pair of sewing scissors are useful for snipping threads, trimming seams, and cutting applique pieces.

Needles For hand piecing and applique, select the size needle that you find comfortable to use. For embroidery, select a crewel needle with an eye large enough to fit the embroidery thread. For quilting, choose a 'between' needle, also with an eye that will fit the thread you are using. (Generally size 8 or 9 is used.)

Pins Pins are constantly required for patchwork, to pin the pieces together ready for sewing, to pin strips and borders to blocks, and to pin quilts (or parts of quilts) ready for quilting. Glass-headed pins or berry pins are handy to use, and are easier to see when accidentally dropped.

Thimble Quilting is nearly impossible without a thimble. It is a necessary protection for your finger as you push the needle through the three layers of the quilt sandwich. Choose a thimble that fits your finger without being uncomfortably tight, or dropping off too easily. Some people like to use two thimbles when quilting, one on the traditional third finger of the sewing hand, and another on the pointer finger of the other hand. Alternatively, instead of a second thimble, the pointer finger can be protected by a leather thimble, or piece of elastoplast.

Iron As the patchwork pieces are stitched together, each seam needs to be carefully pressed so that the next piece to be seamed will fit accurately, and the block will sit flat. Do not iron too vigorously, or the patchwork will become stretched and distorted — just press gently. Steam pressing will help if stubborn creases occur, or seams don't sit flat. Always press your finished patchwork well before you put the three layers together ready for quilting — after you have added the batting, you will not be able to iron it again!

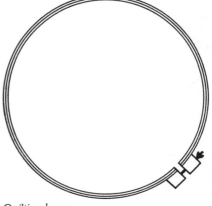

Quilting hoop

Brown paper   A sheet of brown paper, approximately 40 cm (16″) square, is useful for laying out the pieces of your block after you have cut them out. The pieces can be pinned to the paper so they stay in place if you need to carry the block around, or if you cannot do the sewing right away.

Sandpaper   A sheet of fine sandpaper is very useful to position underneath the fabric when marking around a template. The sandpaper prevents the fabric from slipping under the template, particularly when you are marking small pieces. Glue the sandpaper to a piece of thick cardboard or thin chipboard to make it more solid and durable.

Pencils   Sharp HB pencils are needed to draw the design, and mark light-coloured fabrics. Use a white or yellow coloured pencil to mark dark coloured fabrics. You will also need a set of coloured pencils for colouring the block designs, so you can match the correct template with a particular piece of fabric. (Crayons or textas can be used instead of pencils.)

Ruler   A ruler is necessary for drawing the designs on to graph paper when making templates. A ruler is also used when marking fabric ready to be cut into strips for borders or strips between blocks.

Glue stick   When making templates, use a glue stick to paste your drawn design onto cardboard.

Masking tape   Masking tape is useful for marking straight lines when you are quilting.

Materials for Patchwork

Fabrics   The most suitable fabrics for patchwork are cotton, and cotton-polyester mix fabrics with a firm and even weave. You can use poplin, polypoplin, calico, homespun, lawn — in fact, most dress-weight fabrics. Other fabrics can be used, but may be more difficult to sew. A good quality cotton lawn is highly suitable for the backing layer of the quilt, as it is soft and easy to quilt. Cotton lawn is also ideal for small applique pieces, such as eyes and claws.

Prewash and iron all the fabrics before you use them, to safeguard against colour running and shrinkage.

Selecting colours   Choose coloured fabrics which will most suit your project. The designs can be made in naturalistic colours, and suggestions for suitable colours have been made for each block. Remember these are only suggestions — feel free to use your own ideas. For a bold and different effect, bright non-naturalistic colours can also be used. Select either prints or plain-coloured fabrics (or combinations of both), depending on your taste. Prints can be used most effectively to suggest textures, such as the prickles of the Echidna, or the feathers of the Kookaburra. Plain fabrics will show up quilting designs more than print fabrics.

Always keep in mind that good patchwork should contain a variety of tones — that is, there should be a variety of light and dark in the colours used. If fabrics are all of the one tone they will look dull together, even though the colours may be different. For instance, if you make the Koala in a grey colour, as a contrast, you might choose a light colour for the tree trunk.

Batting   Polyester batting is the most widely available and practical material for the padding layer in quilting. It comes in a variety of different thicknesses, so choose a thickness suitable for your project. For instance, choose a thin batting for clothing but, for a quilt, choose a thicker one. Do not choose very thick batting, as it will be almost impossible to sew when the time comes to quilt. If you want a very flat look to your quilting, cotton flannelette (well preshrunk) or thin wool blanketing can be substituted for the polyester batting.

Threads

Threads for piecing: For both hand piecing and machine piecing, use a good quality machine sewing thread. If you are using the machine, white thread can be used throughout but, if you are hand piecing, match the thread to the darker of the two fabrics to be sewn together.

Threads for hand quilting: Quilting requires a strong thread that will not break easily with the constant rubbing through the eye of the needle. For hand quilting, use the quilting thread made especially for this purpose. Quilting thread comes in a limited range of colours, so you can either select a colour, or stay with the more traditional white or cream.

Threads for machine quilting: For machine quilting, use a good quality machine sewing thread. Match the top thread to the colour of your patchwork, and the bobbin thread to the colour of the backing fabric. Clear polyester thread is an alternative top thread, as it will blend into all colours. (Use it on the top only, and use an ordinary thread on the bobbin.)

Threads for embroidery: Stranded embroidery thread can be used to embroider the details of animals, such as claws and whiskers. Use two threads of the stranded cotton together (or more, if you want a thicker thread.)

Graph paper Large sheets of graph paper (size A2 or A3) are needed to draw the designs for your templates. Each design will need a 24 cm (9") square of paper.

Cardboard Pieces of cardboard about 25 cm (10") square will be needed to make the templates. Choose cardboard that is firm but will not be too difficult to cut with scissors (a little heavier than a cereal packet is ideal). For applique, you will need small pieces of lightweight cardboard, such as the backs of greeting cards.

Australian animal and bird quilt, machine pieced by Judy Turner and hand quilted by the author. Eighteen block designs sewn together with strips of background fabric between them. The blocks in alternate rows were centred in the spaces of the row above, to give a stepped effect.

Vest and bag made by Kerry Gavin. The colourful vest, made with bound edges, features the Koala on the back and the Wallaby on the front. The bag uses the Platypus design. Both were machine pieced and hand quilted.

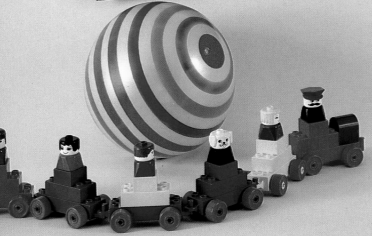

Platypus and Frog quilt, machine pieced and hand quilted by Trudy Brodie. Clever use of fabrics in bright primary colours makes this stunning quilt. Charming motifs were quilted into spaces on the blocks and borders.

Blue wren wallhanging, machine pieced and hand quilted by Wendy Saclier. Three wrens, scaled to different sizes and facing opposite directions, combine to make a pretty hanging.

How to Make Patchwork Blocks

Making the templates

Step 1: Copy the design on to graph paper, 1 square = 1 cm (1 square = ⅜"). The finished block size is 24 cm (9").
Note: To enlarge or reduce the design, change the size of the squares (see Figure 3). For instance, to make the block 30 cm (12") square, you could make the squares 12.5 mm (½") instead of 1 cm (⅜") or, to make the block 36 cm (15"), the squares will be 15 mm (⅝"). Draw the grid of squares first, then copy the design.

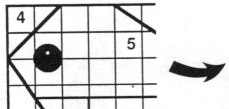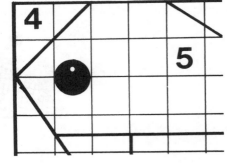

Figure 3. Changing the size of a design.

Step 2: Clearly number each piece, carefully copying from the original design. Mark any notches. The notches have been put on some pieces to help you place them correctly after they have been cut from the fabric.

Step 3: Use appropriate coloured pencils to colour all the pieces of the design which are not background pieces. This does not have to be a beautiful colouring job — just enough to give you an idea of the colour for each piece. This step will help you to select the right fabric when the templates have all been cut out.

Step 4: Use the glue stick to paste the graph paper design on to a square of cardboard. Cut out each numbered piece. Because you began with a square, which was then cut up, you know that the pieces *must* fit together again to make the block.

Step 5: Mark the grain line on the *underside* of each template. This step is necessary because, when you are marking the fabrics, the template will actually be face down. The grain of the fabric in your block should run in the same direction as the lines on your graph paper, so use these lines to help mark the grain line. In the case of most templates, one or more of the edges of the template will be on one of the lines of the graph-paper grid, so a line can simply be marked parallel to one of these edges (see Figure 4).

Figure 4. Marking the grain line on the underside of the template.

(a) One edge of the template is on one of the graph grid lines.

(b) Turn the template over, and mark the grain line parallel to the edge which was on the grid line.

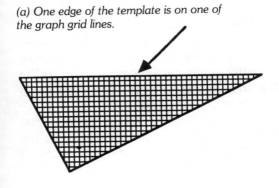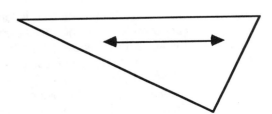

For templates which do not have one edge on a grain line, take a pin and poke it twice through the template along any line of the graph-paper grid, making the holes a little distance apart. Turn the template over, and draw a line between the two holes. This will give you a grain line (see Figure 5). Also mark the position of any *notches* on the underside of the template.

Figure 5. Marking the grain line on the underside of the template when one side of the template is not on the graph grid.

(a) Push pins through the cardboard at two points along a line on the graph paper.

(b) Turn the template over and draw a line between the two pin holes.

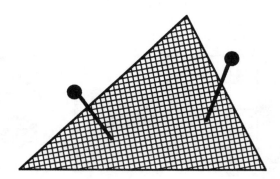
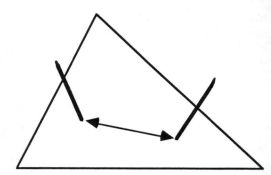

Marking the fabric

Step 1: For the finished design to turn out the same way it is facing in the diagram, you will need to turn the templates *face down* as you mark the fabric. Of course there may be times when you deliberately want the animal to face the opposite way, so in these cases use the templates face up.

Step 2: Use a sharp pencil to draw around each cardboard piece (face down, remember!) on to appropriately coloured fabric. Use a lead pencil for light fabrics, and a white or yellow pencil for dark fabrics. Make sure your pencil is really sharp, and sharpen it frequently, so that the pieces are not marked bigger than they ought to be because of a thick pencil line. Leave about 2 cm (½″) between the pieces, to leave space for the seam allowances. The pencil line you have marked will be your *sewing line*. Placing sandpaper under your fabric before you mark it will prevent the fabric from slipping under the template (this is especially useful for small pieces).

Cutting and laying out the pieces

Step 1: Cut out each piece, leaving 6 mm (¼″) around your marked lines for a seam allowance. Do *not* cut on the marked lines, as these are your sewing lines.

Step 2: As you cut out each piece, lay it in its correct place on your square of brown paper. Keep the original design in front of you, to check where each piece should go. Also use any notches to help you place the pieces in the correct orientation to each other. At this stage, the pieces will appear not to fit together, but this is due to the seam allowances — they will fit accurately when they are sewn together. If you can't sew the pieces straight away, pin the pieces to the brown paper.

The importance of laying out the pieces in their correct places cannot be stressed enough. This avoids confusion when sewing the pieces together. Always replace the pieces in their correct position once they have been joined together, continually referring back to the diagram.

How to sew the pieces together

Step 1: Pin the pieces together before sewing. Pick up the two pieces you wish to join, put them right sides together, then poke pins through each end of the line along which you are going to stitch. Pull gently on the seam line to align the pencil lines marked on both pieces, then put pins along the seam line. Check both sides to make certain that the pins are going exactly along the marked lines. Add several pins at right angles to the line (see Figure 6).

Figure 6. Pin the patchwork pieces together before sewing.

(a) Poke pins through both pieces at the corners of the lines; (b) pin along the marked line; (c) add pins at right angles to the marked line.

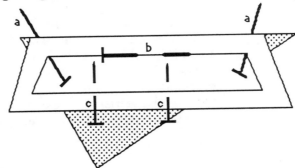

Step 2: Stitch along the marked line, removing the pins just before you come to them. Check both sides of your work after sewing, to be sure the stitching is on the marked lines.

If you are machine stitching, begin your stitching at the cut edges of the pieces, stitch across the seam allowance, and along the line to the other cut edges of the pieces (see Figure 7). Trim the ends of the threads as you go.

Figure 7.

Machine stitching goes from cut edge to cut edge, along the marked line.

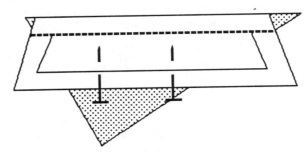

If you are hand piecing, use a small running stitch. Sew only along the marked line, beginning with a knot and a back stitch, and ending with a couple of back stitches (see Figure 8).

Figure 8.

When hand piecing, the stitching follows the marked lines, and does not go across the seam allowances.

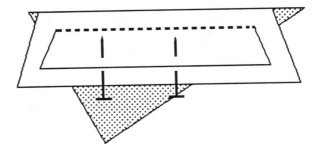

Step 3: Press each seam after stitching. Press the seam allowances to one side, preferably the side of the darkest fabric.

Step 4: After sewing and pressing, remember to place each unit back in its correct position on your sheet of brown paper.

Step 5: Continue sewing all the pieces together until the block is complete. Press the block well.

The sewing order

The sewing order (also called the piecing order) has been carefully planned for each block, so that it is the easiest way to put the block together, and so that all the seams involve straight sewing, with the minimum matching of seams. For simplicity and ease of sewing, it is very important that you follow the sewing order given for each block. As you sew, keep the diagram and instructions for each block nearby, so they can be referred to continually. Think of the sewing order as you would a knitting pattern — complete each row in the order given. When knitting, you don't do row six of the knitting pattern before you do row three! Mistakes will not occur in patchwork either if you follow the steps carefully.

The numbers in the sewing order refer to the number given to each piece of template in the original diagram. For instance in the Koala design, piece number 1 is the triangle shape that forms part of the right ear, piece number 2 is the background above the head, and piece number 3 is part of the left ear (see Figure 9).

The symbol + means to sew the two pieces together — so the direction for sewing pieces 1 and 2 together will look like this:

    1 + 2

For the Koala, the first instruction says:

    1 1 + 2 + 3

This means, for step one, you sew piece 1 to piece 2, then add piece 3.

Once pieces have been joined together, the numbers are put into brackets, indicating that those pieces are now a unit. If there are just two pieces in the unit, it will be described as (1,2). If there are three pieces in the unit, as in the second step of the Koala, it will be described as (1-3). Seven pieces in the unit would make it (1-7), and so on.

Pieces can then be added to an already sewn unit. Again using the example of the Koala, the directions continue:

    2 (1-3) + 4

Thus, in step two, piece 4 is added to the unit made of pieces 1, 2 and 3.

Sometimes the instructions direct you to leave aside the previously sewn unit or units, and to pick up other pieces of the design and begin sewing them into a unit. In the Koala, pieces 5 and 6 must be joined together before they are added to the unit made from pieces 1, 2, 3, and 4. So the directions continue:

    3 5 + 6
    4 (1-4) + (5,6) + 7.

The unit of 1, 2, 3, and 4 is thus sewn to the unit of 5 and 6, and then piece 7 added. This whole section is now called (1-7).

The directions continue step-by-step until all the pieces have been joined together.

Figure 9. Koala sewing order: the first six steps illustrated.

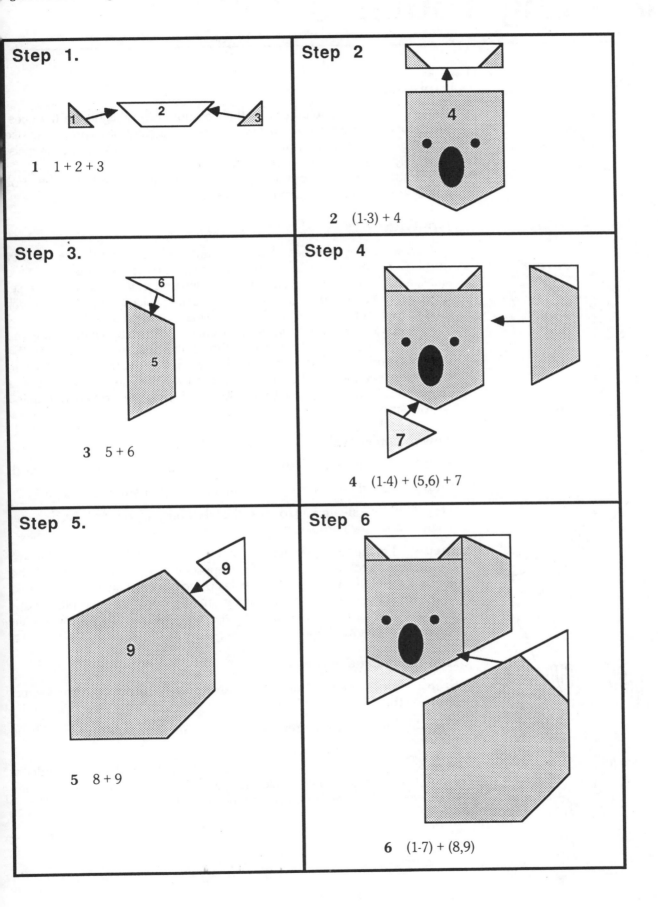

Step 1.

1   1 + 2 + 3

Step 2

2   (1-3) + 4

Step 3.

3   5 + 6

Step 4

4   (1-4) + (5,6) + 7

Step 5.

5   8 + 9

Step 6

6   (1-7) + (8,9)

Finishing Touches

Figure 10. Stitches

Running stitch

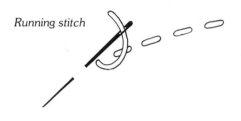

Satin stitch

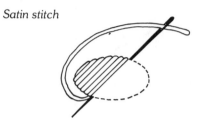

Stem stitch

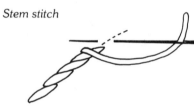

Chain stitch

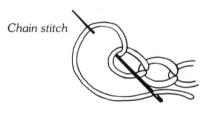

Long and short stitch

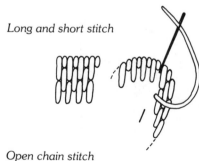

Open chain stitch

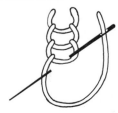

Embroidery

Details, such as the whiskers on the Possum and highlights on the eyes, need to be embroidered on the blocks. You may also prefer to use embroidery, rather than applique, to add other details of the animals, especially when the details are small.

Use stranded thread for the embroidery, using two strands at a time. For a thicker line, increase the number of strands.

Appliqué

Details, such as eyes, noses, claws, etc. can be added by hand applique after the block has been sewn together. Because many of the applique pieces are small, a finely woven fabric, e.g. good quality cotton lawn, is very suitable. Other fabrics can be used, but if they have a high polyester content they will tend to fray more easily and will not sit nicely when pressed flat.

Most shapes, such as squares and triangles, can be appliqued using the general method below. Use this method for shapes like the nose of the Wombat, and the throat of the Frilled lizard. Special instructions are given for circles (see Figure 11), so follow these to make eyes for many of the animals and birds. Claws can be appliqued following the method for making narrow strips.

How to appliqué shapes (general method)

Step 1: The shape you want to applique must be cut out of thin cardboard.

Step 2: Cut the fabric 6 mm (¼″) larger than the cardboard shape.

Step 3: Use a steam iron to press the fabric around the cardboard shape. Then remove the cardboard.

Step 4: Pin the applique shape in place and hand stitch in position, using a thread that matches the colour of the applique piece. The stitching will be almost invisible if you bring your needle up and out through the pressed fold of the applique shape... then push it straight down into the patchwork block... and bring it back up into the fold again... then down again through the block... and so on.

How to appliqué narrow strips

Step 1: Cut strips of fabric on the bias, 8 mm (⅜″) wider than the desired finished strip.

Step 2: Finger press under a 4 mm (⅛″) seam allowance on each side of the strip.

Step 3: Cut the strip to the length required plus 8 mm (⅜″). Turn under a 4 mm (⅛″) seam allowance at each end, and applique in place. Because the strips were cut on the bias, they can be curved.

How to appliqué circles (see Figure 11)

Step 1: Cut a cardboard circle the size desired for your finished applique piece.

Step 2: Cut a circle of fabric 8 mm (⅜″) larger than the piece of cardboard. Hand sew a line of small running stitches around the outside of the fabric circle, and leave the end of the thread dangling.

Step 3: Place the cardboard circle inside the circle of fabric, on the wrong side of the fabric. Pull the thread of your running stitches, which will gather the fabric around the cardboard circle. Use a steam iron to press well, with the gathered side upwards. Loosen the running stitching, and remove the cardboard. Using a sharp pair of scissors, trim away the extra seam allowance (including your stitching), so that the seam allowance is now only 4 mm (⅛″).

Step 4: Pin the circle in place, and hand stitch (as described in Step 4 of the general method outlined on the facing page).

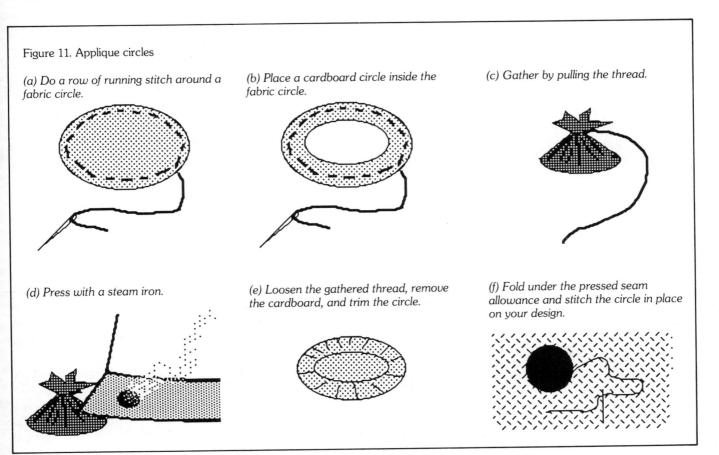

Figure 11. Applique circles

(a) Do a row of running stitch around a fabric circle.

(b) Place a cardboard circle inside the fabric circle.

(c) Gather by pulling the thread.

(d) Press with a steam iron.

(e) Loosen the gathered thread, remove the cardboard, and trim the circle.

(f) Fold under the pressed seam allowance and stitch the circle in place on your design.

How to Quilt

Figure 12. Quilting designs.

Quilting designs (see Figure 12)

Step 1: The block designs in this book can be quilted with outline quilting which follows the lines of the patchwork. The quilting can be 'in the ditch' (which means it is almost on top of the seam) or it can be a small distance away from the seam. Quilting patterns can be used within shapes, to create backgrounds, and to decorate borders, strips, or spaces between blocks. For instance, semi-circles can be used to create the patterns of feathers on the birds, or leaf shapes can be quilted around borders. Geometric patterns, such as lines and grids, are always effective.

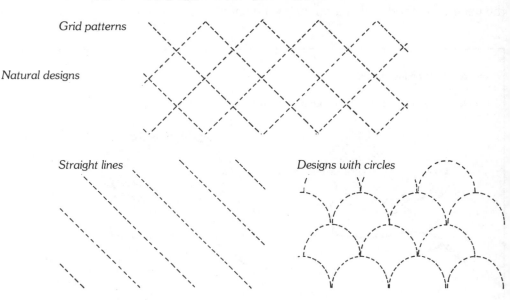

Grid patterns

Natural designs

Straight lines   *Designs with circles*

Step 2: Quiting designs need to be marked on to the patchwork top before the three layers are put together for quilting. Use a sharp pencil, and mark very lightly. Straight-line designs can be drawn with a ruler. To repeat patterns, cut shapes from cardboard, then draw around them. For instance, to repeat a pattern of gum leaves and nuts, first draw the design on to paper, then paste it on cardboard and cut it out. Place the cardboard shape wherever you want the quilting design to be, and lightly draw around it.

Masking tape can be used when quilting straight line patterns. The advantage of using masking tape is that you do not need to mark the patchwork top with a pencil. Use the tape after the three layers of the quilt are tacked (basted) together. Lay a strip of masking tape so that one edge follows the line where you want the quilting to be. Quilt along beside the masking tape. The strip of tape can then be removed, and placed in position for your next line. You will be able to use the same strip of tape several times. Masking tape can be used both for hand quilting and machine quilting.

Quilting by hand

Preparation for hand quilting

Step 1: Press the patchwork top thoroughly. Use pencil to lightly mark the quilting design.

Step 2: Prepare a backing fabric. Join lengths of fabric together, if necessary, to make the size you need. Use a soft fabric, such as lawn which will be easy to sew. Plain fabrics show up the quilting, print fabrics tend to hide it. Make the backing about 5 cm (2″) larger than the patchwork top. Press the backing fabric.

Step 3: Cut a piece of batting the same size as the backing fabric. For larger quilts, the batting may need to be joined. Butt the cut edges of the batting together, and loosely stitch by hand, using a whip stitch.

Step 4: Lay the backing fabric down smoothly (right side down). Smooth the batting over the backing, then lay the patchwork on the top (right side up). Make sure there are *no wrinkles* in any of the three layers.

Step 5: Pin the three layers together, placing pins about 10 cm-15 cm (4″-6″) apart. Check the backing at this stage, to be sure there are no wrinkles. Use a long needle and large stitches to tack (baste) the three layers together. Tack in a grid, with lines of stitching about 10 cm-15 cm (4″-6″) apart.

Step 6: Lay the inner ring of your quilting hoop down, smooth the prepared quilt on top, then push on the outer ring of the hoop. The three layers of the quilt sandwich are now held firmly in place, ready for you to quilt. Begin quilting at the centre of your quilt. Quilt the space held in the hoop, then move the hoop to the next unquilted space. Do not jump from place to place at random, but move systematically from already quilted parts to unquilted parts.

Hand quilting

Step 1: Hand quilting is simply a running stitch joining the three layers of the quilt sandwich together. However, it does take a little practice to get the stitches even (see Figure 13).

Step 2: Thread a 'between' needle (size 8 or 9) with quilting thread, making the thread no longer than 45 cm (18″). Tie a knot in the end of the thread.

Step 3: Put a thimble on the middle finger of your sewing hand, and protect the pointer finger of your other hand with another thimble or with elastoplast. Rest the hoop comfortably on a table, or on the arms of a chair, so that both your hands are free.

Step 4: Push the needle up through your quilt, at the place where you want to start, then tug gently on the thread to pull the knot into the batting. Don't be too vigorous, or it will pull through all three layers! Make a small back stitch to anchor the thread firmly. Place your pointer finger just below where you are stitching, push the needle through the quilt so that the tip of the needle just grazes the top of the finger underneath. Rock the point of the needle upwards, and bring it out so that you have made a small stitch. Your thimble should be behind the needle, pushing it. With practice you will soon find that you are able to make more than one stitch at a time. The stitching must go through all three layers — which is why the pointer finger of the hand beneath the quilting may need some protection! End your stitching with a small back stitch, then make a long stitch through into the layer of batting. Bring the thread up to the top and snip it off.

Quilting is easiest at places where there are no underlying seam allowances. Where the inevitable bulk from a seam junction occurs you may have to quilt just one stitch at a time, sometimes even making each stitch with a single downward motion followed by a single upward motion.

Figure 13.

The quilting stitch is a running stitch that goes through all three layers of the quilt sandwich. It takes two hands, one above, and one below the quilt.

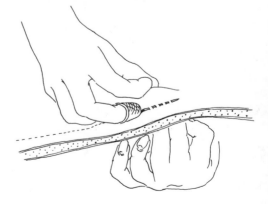

Machine quilting

Step 1: Machine quilting is ideal for small objects, such as cot quilts, cushions and bags. Large quilts cannot be manoeuvered under the arm of the sewing machine, so they must be constructed and quilted in manageable sections. The sections can be quilted, and then joined together after the quilting. The joins on the back of the quilt can be covered with strips of fabric.

Step 2: Prepare the quilt layers in the manner described above for hand quilting but, instead of tacking (basting) the layers together, it is only necessary to pin them.

Step 3: Set up your sewing machine so that you will have a good space to your left. On the top use thread to match your patchwork, and on the bobbin use thread to match your backing fabric. Set the stitch length to about 2½.

Step 4: Stitch 'in the ditch' of the seam, or along the lines you have marked for a quilting design. When you are stitching 'in the ditch', it is easiest to sew along the side which has not had the seam allowances pressed to lay under it. If it is necessary to stitch along the side where the seam allowances are, it is neater and easier to stitch slightly to one side. Begin and end your stitching with a couple of back stitches, and trim thread ends neatly.

Step 5: If you are joining sections of a quilt that have already been machine quilted, first seam the sections to each other, right sides together. Trim away the batting in the seam allowances so there is no extra bulk. Cut strips of fabric on the straight of the grain, 5 cm (2") wide and the length necessary to cover all the seams. (You may have to join some strips together.) Fold both lengthwise edges of the strips into the centre, and press in position. Pin, and hand stitch the strips in place over the seam allowances on the back of the quilt.

How to make a quilt

Requirements

• *Fabric*, for the patchwork top. For the animal and bird blocks you will require an assortment of small pieces in suitable colours, as well as fabric for the background of the blocks. You also need fabric for strips, borders, and binding, as indicated in your quilt plan. The quantity of fabrics will vary depending on the size of the quilt, and the block (or blocks) chosen. Remember to add seam allowances when making your estimate.

• *Batting*, the size of your finished patchwork top, plus 5 cm (2″) all around.

• *Backing fabric*, the same size as your finished patchwork top, plus 5 cm (2″) all around. Lengths of fabric may have to be joined (by machine) to make the required size. Choose a fabric that is soft and easy to quilt.

• *Threads*. You will need suitable threads for piecing, applique and/or embroidery, tacking (basting) and quilting.

Making the quilt

The steps in making a quilt are the same whether the quilt is a large one for a bed, or a small one for a cot or to be used as a wall hanging.

Step 1: Choose the block designs you are going to use, and plan how you will make them into a quilt. You may wish to use all the designs, some of the designs, or just one design repeated in different ways.

To introduce variety into your quilt, you can make the animals or birds look in the opposite direction by marking the fabric with templates *face up* instead of face down. The blocks can be put together in many ways (see Figure 15 on page 25). For instance, they can be sewn with strips of fabric in between, or the pieced blocks can be alternated with blocks of plain fabric. The blocks can have extra borders added to them, either matching the background or in a contrasting colour. To give a stepped effect, the blocks in alternate rows of the quilt can be centred on the spaces between the blocks in the row above. Other patchwork designs can be introduced into the alternate blocks, strips or borders — use your imagination to create your own design.

If your quilt is to fit a particular bed, measure the bed carefully first, in order to make the quilt the right size. Make the patchwork top a few centimetres (about 1″) larger than the finished quilt needs to be, because quilting will take in a little of the size.

Make a simple plan of your quilt on a piece of graph paper, showing where the blocks, strips and borders will be. You may not necessarily follow the plan in every detail, but this step always provides you with a good starting point.

Step 2: Estimate the fabric you need. First, measure the strips and borders, not forgetting to include the seam allowances. Then estimate what you need for the blocks and the amount of backing, batting, and fabric for the final binding. Always overestimate your requirements — it is disastrous to run out before you have finished.

Step 3: Choose and purchase your fabrics. To help you arrive at a satisfying colour combinaton, it is a good idea to group the fabrics together when you are buying them, or carry around samples of ones you have already bought. Don't forget to have variety in the colour tones (lightness and darkness). Prewash and press your fabrics.

Step 4: Draw the designs and make your cardboard templates, (see page 13).

Step 5: Mark your fabrics, and cut out the pieces for the blocks. Lay out the pieces for the blocks in their correct places (see page 14).

Step 6: Sew the blocks, following the sewing order given (see page 16).

Step 7: Cut the fabric for the strips and borders. Construct the quilt top, sewing the strips to the blocks, and adding borders as indicated in your plan.

Step 8: Press the quilt top well, and mark any quilting designs. Prepare the backing and batting for quilting. Pin and tack (baste) the three layers together.

Step 9: Quilt (see page 20). Trim away excess batting and backing from the edge of the quilt.

Step 10: Finish the edges by:
    i) *binding the edges with strips of fabric.* The strips can be cut on the bias (useful if you need to curve around the corners), or cut on the straight of the grain. Measure your quilt across the centre (both lengthwise and crosswise) and make strips equal to these lengths, plus enough to tuck in neatly over the binding at each end. (Measuring the quilt through the centre is more accurate than measuring the sides, which may have become stretched.)
    Strips of fabric folded double make a neat and strong edge. Cut the strips four times the width required for the finished binding, plus 12 mm (½″) for seam allowances — strips cut 8 cm (3″) are a good width. Fold the strips in half lengthwise, and press. Pin the strips to the right side of the edge of the quilt, aligning the raw edges of the strips with the edge of the quilt. Machine stitch in place. Fold the strips to the back of the quilt, tucking the ends neatly over the corners. Hand stitch strips to the back of the quilt (see Figure 14).

Figure 14.

a) The folded strips are stitched to the edge of the quilt, raw edges together.

b) The strips are then folded to the back of the quilt, and hand stitched in place.

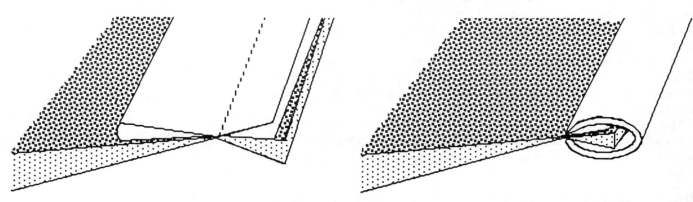

    ii) *bringing the top of the quilt to the back.* Fold the top of the quilt to the the back, turn under a small seam allowance, and hand stitch in place. Note that when using this method, extra fabric needs to be added to the patchwork top so that there will be enough to fold to the back.

Figure 15. Designing with quilt blocks.

a) Reversing the block.

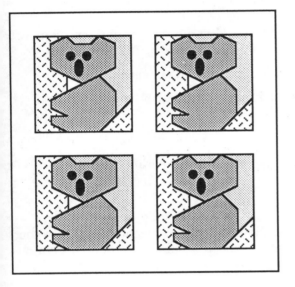

b) Blocks with strips between.

d) Blocks with alternate rows stepped.

c) Pieced blocks alternated with plain blocks.

e) Block with two borders.

How to make a cushion

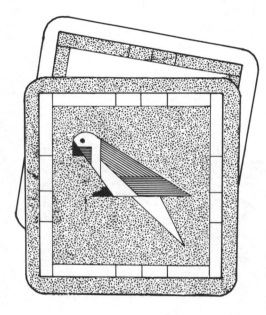

Requirements

- *Finished patchwork block*, made to the size you require with borders — about 45 cm (18″) is a good size. (The suggested requirements below are for this size.) To make the patchwork top you need:
  — small pieces of a variety of fabrics, to make the animal or bird
  — 30 cm (12″) of fabric for the background
  — 30 cm (12″) of fabric for borders. (For more than one border you may want to have several different fabrics to make up this amount.)

- *Fabric*, 50 cm (20″), for back of cushion and binding.

- *Batting*, a square the size of the finished patchwork block, plus 3 cm (1″) all around — about 50 cm (20″) square.

- *Backing fabric*, a square the same size as the batting, for the quilting.

- *Zip*, 5 cm (2″) shorter than the width of the finished cushion — 40 cm (16″).

Making the cushion

Step 1:   Tack (baste) the backing, batting and patchwork top together, and quilt. Trim away the extra batting and backing, and round the corners slightly so that the cushion will not have pointy 'ears'.

Step 2:   Cut the fabric for the back of the cushion, making it the same width as the quilted block, but 5 cm (2″) longer, to allow for the zipper insertion.

Step 3:   Insert zipper across the centre of the cushion back, using the extra length to make seam allowances for the zipper.

Step 4:   From the remainder of the fabric for the cushion back, cut bias strips 4 cm (1½″) wide. Join the strips together to make a length about 2 m (2 yds) long.

Step 5:   Assemble the cushion. Lay out the back of the cushion, right side facing downward. Lay the quilted top over this, right side up. Pin layers together. Pin bias strip around the outside of the cushion, tucking in the ends neatly where they join. Machine stitch the bias strip to the cushion (you will be stitching on the right side of the cushion).

Step 6:   Finger press a small seam allowance on the bias strip. Fold it over to the back of the cushion and hand stitch it in place.

How to make a bag

Requirements

- *Two blocks of patchwork,* with borders added to make the desired size — about 40 cm (16") is a good size. (The requirements listed below are for this size.)
- *Fabric,* 70 cm (28") to make bag lining and handles.
- *Batting,* 50 cm (20")
- *Backing fabric,* 50 cm (20")

Making the bag

Step 1: Cut the fabric for lining the bag into two squares the same size as your finished patchwork squares. Cut two strips 10 cm (3½") wide by 46 cm (18") long, for the handles.

Step 2: Cut the batting into two squares, each 3 cm (1") larger all around than the patchwork squares. Cut two strips of batting, 4 cm (1½") wide and 46 cm (18") long, to line the handles.

Step 3: Cut the backing fabric into two squares, each the same size as the batting.

Step 4: Using the batting and backing, assemble the two patchwork squares ready for quilting. Quilt by hand or machine. Trim away excess batting and backing.

Step 5: Pin the quilted squares with right sides together. Stitch around the two sides and the bottom, making a 6 mm (¼") seam. Turn the bag right side out.

Step 6: Iron 6 mm (¼") seam allowances down on each side of the strips of fabric intended for the handles. Fold the strips in half lengthwise, and iron again. Insert the strips of batting into the fold and, stitching near the edges, stitch down each side of the handles.

Step 7: Pin the handles in place on the outside of the bag, with the raw edges of the handles even with the raw edges of the top of the bag. Stitch the handles in place.

Step 8: Pin the two squares of lining fabric together. Stitch down both sides and part way across the base, leaving a 20 cm (8") opening unstitched at the centre of the base. Sew these seams a little wider than the ones you used to join the quilted squares, so that the lining will fit snugly into the bag. Do not turn the lining right side out.

Step 9: Fit the lining over the bag, and pin it in place. The right sides of the lining should be against the right sides of the bag. Stitch around the top of the bag. Turn the bag right side out through the opening in the lining. Slip stitch the opening closed.

Step 10: Push the lining into the bag, then sew a line of stitching a little distance down from the top of the bag, to hold the lining in place.

Vests and Clothing

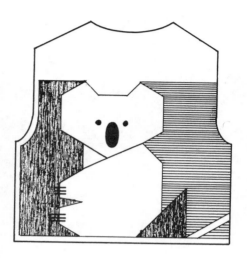

Vests

To look good, vests must fit well. It is, therefore, a good idea to use some unwanted fabric and make a mock-up of your vest pattern. You can try this on the person for whom the vest is intended. Use this trial to make any necessary adjustments to the pattern, such as cutting bigger armholes, lengthening, shortening, or taking in the side seams. Use thin, firm batting to interline the vest, or else use flannelette which will give it body, without making it too thick.

Vest with bound edges

Requirements

• *Commercial pattern* for a vest in the desired size. Choose a simple pattern without darts.

• *Fabric,* for the animals or birds an assortment of small pieces is needed. You also need an amount for the background of the blocks and an amount, according to the pattern, for the remainder of the vest. A women's size vest will need approximately 80 cm (30″) of fabric 115 cm (45″) wide, and a child's vest will need proportionately less. For the lining, you will also need an amount according to the pattern.

• *Thin batting,* or cotton flannelette (prewashed), for interlining — same size as the fabric for lining.

• *Bias strips,* or 25 mm (1″) purchased bias binding. If you are making your own bias strips, they should be cut 4 cm (1½″) wide, and extra fabric will be required for this. About 30 cm (12″) should be sufficient. The length of the binding needs to be the same as the perimeter of the vest, including armholes — about 4 m (4½ yds) for an adult size.

Making the vest

Step 1:   Choose the block designs you wish to use, and make them up. Add extra fabric all around each block to make it of sufficient size for your pattern pieces. Cut out the vest pieces.

Step 2:   Cut interlining and lining, 3 cm (1″) larger than the vest pieces. For each piece of the vest, assemble all three layers together, and quilt by hand or machine. Trim away excess interlining and lining.

Step 3:   Stitch the quilted pieces of the vest together. Trim seam allowances, and cut away excess batting. Neaten seams on the inside of the shoulders and underarms by covering them with strips of fabric. Cut these strips 3 cm (1¼″) wide, and press a small seam allowance down on each side. Pin the strips over the seams, and hand stitch in place.

Step 4:   Bind the outside of the vest, using the bias strips or purchased bias binding. If you are hand finishing, sew the binding to the right side of the vest, then fold the binding over to the inside and hand stitch in place. To machine finish, stitch the binding to the inside of the vest first, then fold it to the outside and machine stitch in place.

Bird cushions, machine pieced and hand quilted by Kerry Gavin. Colourful Rosellas and Cockatoos contrast against the black backgrounds. Each block was surrounded by three borders: first a black border, then a coloured border (short coloured strips were pieced together for the Rosellas), and finally another black border.

Dress and pinafore by Linda McGuire. Two Blue wrens make a pretty addition to the dainty dress for a four year old, and the Koala block is a delightful decoration for a baby's pinafore. The blocks were machine pieced.

Pelican quilt, machine pieced and machine quilted by Judy Turner.
Four Pelican blocks were repeated in this simple quilt design which gains
its effect from varying the shade of the background colour.

Vests by Kerry Gavin. Two nocturnal creatures, the Possum and the Boobook owl, decorate one vest. The Echidna and Frilled Lizard feature on another which cleverly opens down the centre front. Both vests are machine pieced and hand quilted.

Vest without binding

Requirements

(As for vest with bound edges, except no binding is required.)

Making the vest

Step 1:   Construct the patchwork blocks, add fabric to make them the size required for the vest pieces. Follow your pattern to cut out the vest pieces.

Step 2:   Cut interlining and lining fabric the same size as your vest pieces. Treating each layer separately, stitch the underarm seams for all three layers. Pin layers together, with the right side of the vest facing the right side of the lining, and with the interlining on top of the lining.

Step 3:   Stitch around the edges of the vest, stitching across the back of the neck, around each arm hole, down each front and across the bottom of the vest. *Leave the shoulders unstitched* (see Figure 16).

Figure 16. Constructing vest without binding.

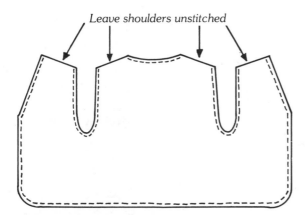

Leave shoulders unstitched

Step 4:   Trim seam allowances, and cut away excess interlining. Turn the vest right side out through one of the shoulders.

Step 5:   Quilt the vest by hand or machine.

Step 6:   Sew the shoulder seams, putting the right sides ogether. Trim seams, and trim away excess interlining. Make two strips of fabric 3 cm (1¼″) wide, and the length of the shoulder seams plus 1 cm (½″) at each end. Press seam allowances down each side of these strips. Neaten the shoulder seams, by hand stitching the strips of fabric over them.

Clothing

Patchwork blocks can be effectively applied to clothing. Find a commercial garment pattern which has an area suitable for placing the patchwork. Yokes, bibs, borders, pockets, and areas on the centre front or centre back of garments are some possibilities. Look for a simple pattern, which has no darts or shaping where the patchwork will be placed. Make a pattern of that area, construct the block or blocks, then add borders to make the block the required size, or trim away any unwanted fabric should the pattern area be less than the block size. Alternatively, blocks can be enlarged or reduced to fit suitable areas (see page 13). If you plan to quilt the garment, use thin batting or flannelette as padding, so that the garment does not become too bulky.

Patterns for the Designs

Koala

PAR

The Koala is a marsupial animal which means it bears its young in a pouch. Its sole diet is the leaves from certain varieties of eucalyptus trees, and it spends most of its life in the treetops.

Colours

- Pieces 1, 3, 4, 5, 9, 13, 15 and 17 — grey.

- Piece 7 — light grey or white.*

- Pieces 2, 6, 8 and 10 — background.

- Pieces 11, 12, 14, 16, 18 and 19 — brown (or suitable colour for a tree).

- Nose, eyes, and claws — black.

  * For a different shape to the neck, piece 7 can be divided in two (see the dotted line on the design), with the top half being made from the background colour, and the lower half from light grey or white.

Sewing order

1 1 + 2 + 3

2 (1-3) + 4

3 5 + 6

4 (1-4) + (5,6) + 7

5 8 + 9

6 (1-7) + (8,9)

7 (1-9) + 10

8 (1-10) + 11

9 12 + 13 + 14 + 15 + 16 + 17 + 18

10 (1-11) + (12-18) + 19

11 Cut eyes and nose from black fabric, and cut short strips of narrow black bias to make claws. Applique these in place.

Koala

1 square = 1 cm (⅜″)

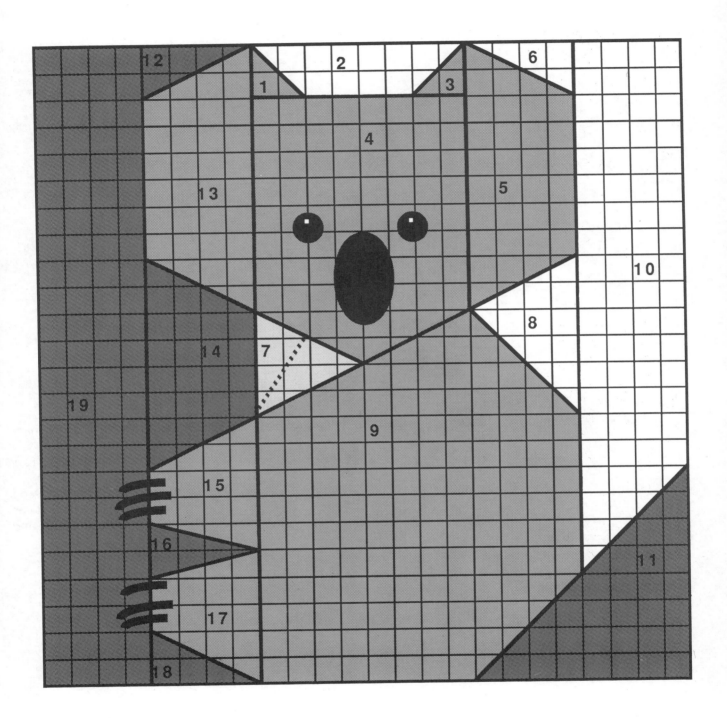

Wombat

The Wombat is a sturdy burrowing marsupial. Different varieties of wombats can be found throughout Australia. They dig deep burrows and generally feed on grass.

Colours

- Pieces 1, 3, 4, 6, 7, 8, 11 and 14 — background.
- Pieces 2, 5, 9, 10, 12 and 13 — brown.
- Eyes and nose — black.
- Left ear — light brown.

Sewing order

1 1 + 2 + 3 + 4

2 5 + 6

3 (1-4) + (5,6)

4 (1-6) + 7

5 8 + 9

6 11 + 12

7 (8,9) + 10 + (11,12) + 13 + 14

8 (1-7) + (8-14)

9 Cut the nose and eye shape from black fabric, and applique them in place. (The eye could also be embroidered.) Using piece 5 as a pattern, cut the left ear from light brown fabric, and applique it in place.

Wombat

1 square = 1 cm (⅜")

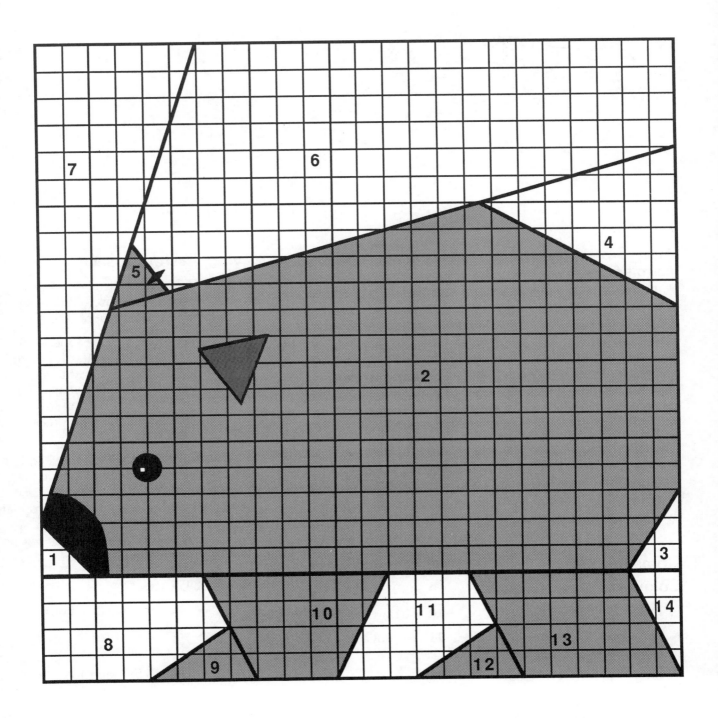

Rosellas

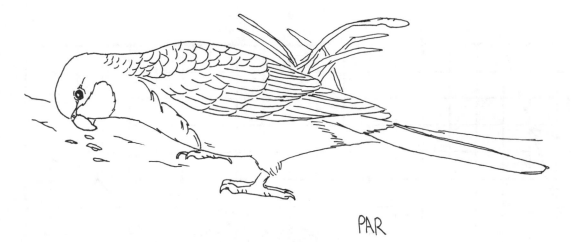

PAR

Eastern rosella and Crimson rosella are two varieties of the many parrots found in Australia. They have brilliantly coloured plumage, and often can be seen in suburban gardens of the south-east.

These two rosellas are made from the same design, but different colours are used. There is also some alteration to several of the pieces for the Eastern rosella. By varying the colours used, it is also possible for you to make other kinds of rosellas, such as the Green rosella or Western rosella.

Crimson rosella

Colours

- Pieces 1 and 3 — bone.
- Pieces 2, 4, 12, 13 and 15 — background.
- Pieces 5, 7, and 11 — red.
- Piece 8 — red and black print, or red with a black quilting design.
- Pieces 6, 9, and 14 — light blue.
- Piece 10 — blue.
- Eye — black.

Sewing order

1 1 + 2 + 3

2 4 + 5

3 6 + 7

4 (4,5) + (6,7)

5 8 + 9 + 10

6 (8-10) + 11

7 (4-7) + (8-11)

8 (1-3) + (4-11) + 12

9 13 + 14 + 15

10 (1-12) + (13-15)

11 Applique or embroider the eye.

Eastern rosella

Follow the general directions for the Crimson rosella, but make variations as described below.

Variation 1   Use adhesive tape to stick the templates for pieces 8 and 9 together next to each other, to make one shape — template 8/9. Step 5 of the piecing order now becomes
8/9 + 10.

Variation 2   Follow the dotted line to cut template 14 into pieces 14a and 14b, and use the pieces separately to mark the appropriate coloured fabric. Join 14a to 14b before doing step 9 in the sewing order.

Colours

- Pieces 1 and 3 — bone.
- Pieces 2, 4, 12, 13, and 15 — background.
- Pieces 5, 7, and 14a — red.
- Piece 6 — white.
- Piece 8/9 — green and black print (or green with a black quilting design).
- Piece 10 — light blue.
- Piece 11 — yellow.
- Piece 14b — green.

Rosella

1 square = 1 cm (⅜″)

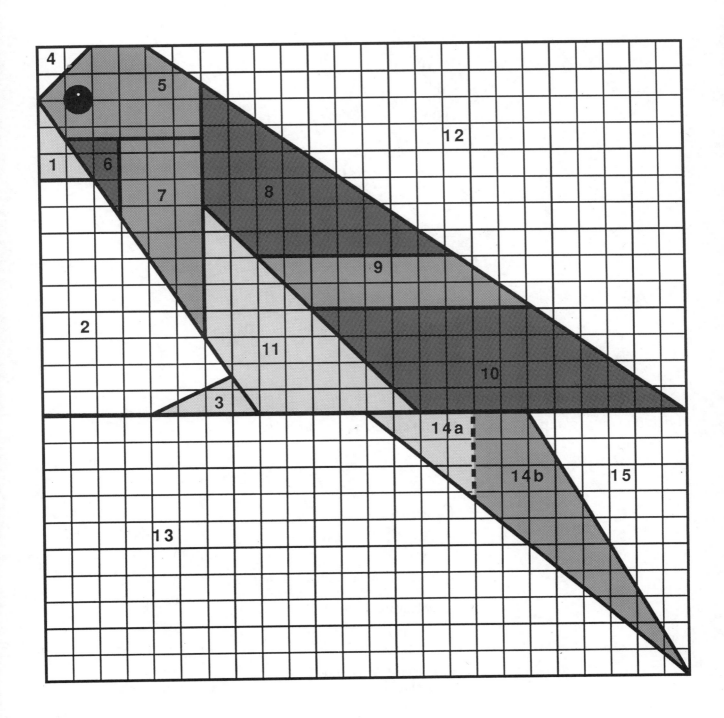

Echidna

The Echidna is an ant-eating animal, with prickly spines on its back and large claws for digging. It is an egglaying mammal like the platypus.

Colours

- Pieces 1, 4, 10 and 13 — brown.
- Pieces 2, 3, 5, 6, 11, 12, 14 and 15 — light brown (or suitable colour for ground).
- Pieces 7 and 16 — brown print or stripe.
- Pieces 8, 9, 17 and 18 — background.
- Eyes, claws and nostrils — black.

Sewing order

1	1 + 2
2	(1,2) + 3
3	4 + 5
4	6 + 7 + 8
5	(1-3) + (4,5) + (6-8) + 9
6	10 + 11
7	(10,11) + 12
8	13 + 14
9	15 + 16 + 17
10	(10-12) + (13,14) + (15-17) + 18
11	(1-9) + (10-18)
12	Applique or embroider the eyes, claws and nostrils.

Echidna

1 square = 1 cm (⅜″)

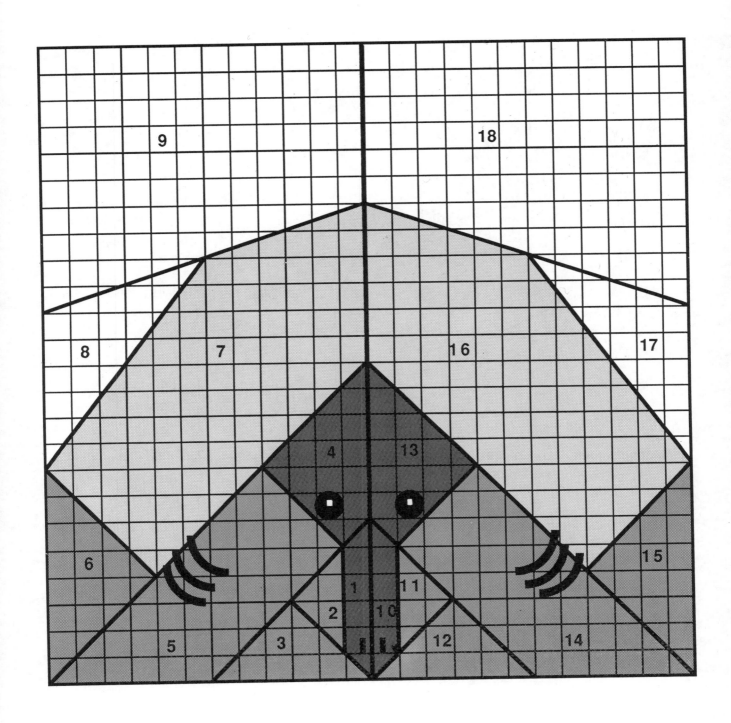

Black swan

The Black swan originally comes from Western Australia, and is the only species of swan native to Australia.

Colours

- Pieces 1, 3, 4, 8 and 10 — black.
- Piece 2 — white.
- Pieces 5, 6, 7, 11, 12, 13 and 14 — background.
- Piece 9 — red.
- Piece 15 — blue (or suitable colour for water).
- Eye — red with a black centre.

Sewing order

1 1 + 2

2 (1,2) + 3

3 (1-3) + 4

4 (1-4) + 5

5 (1-5) + 6

6 (1-6) + 7

7 8 + 9

8 10 + 11

9 (8,9) + (10,11)

10 (8-11) + 12 + 13 + 14

11 (1-7) + (8-14)

12 (1-14) + 15

13 Applique or embroider the eye.

Black swan

1 square = 1 cm (⅜″)

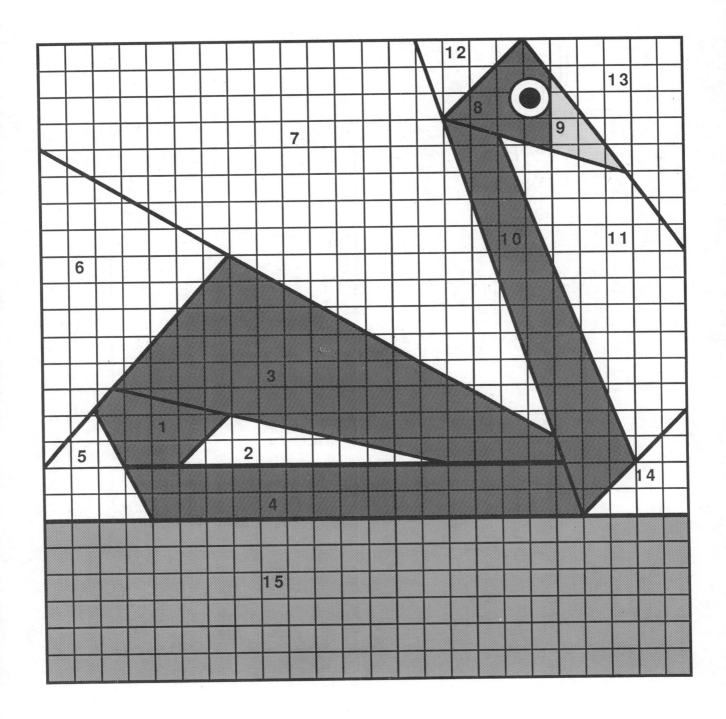

Platypus

The Platypus is a most unusual animal in that it has a duck bill, webbed feet, fur, lays eggs, and suckles its young. It lives in a burrow, but hunts in the water.

Colours

- Pieces 1, 3, 4, 5, 7, 8, 9, 10, 12, 13, 15, 17 and 19 — background.
- Pieces 2, 14, 16, 18 and 20 — dark brown.
- Pieces 6 and 11 — brown.
- Eyes — black.

Sewing order

1 1 + 2 + 3 + 4

2 5 + 6 + 7 + 8 + 9

3 10 + 11 + 12

4 (1-4) + (5-9) + (10-12)

5 13 + 14 + 15 + 16

6 17 + 18 + 19 + 20

7 (1-12) + (13-16) + (17-20)

8 Applique or embroider the eyes.

Platypus

1 square = 1 cm (⅜″)

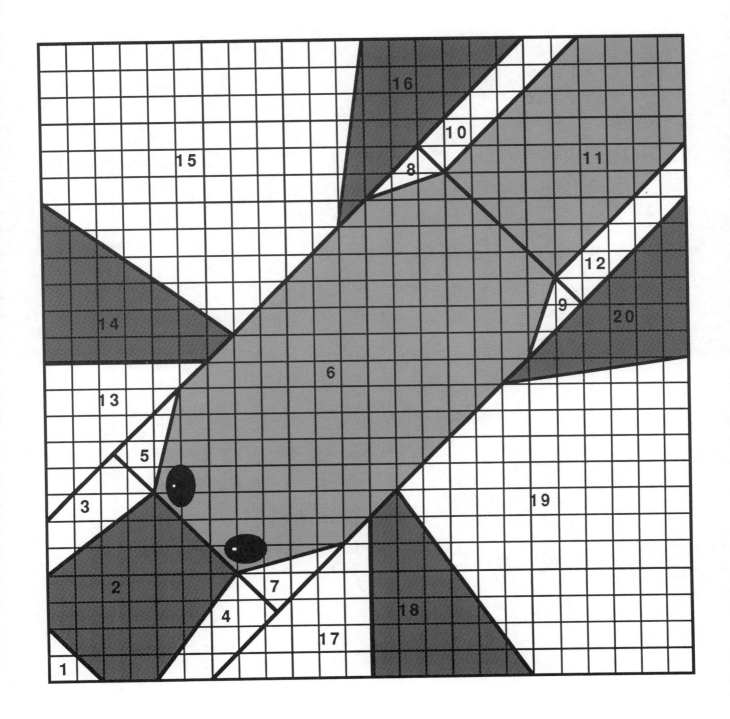

Possum

The Ringtail possum is one of the many varieties of marsupial possum in Australia. It is a nocturnal tree-dwelling animal which lives in the forests of eastern Australia.

Colours

- Pieces 1, 3, 5, 6, 8, 13, 15, 17, 18, 20, 22 and 23 — background.
- Pieces 2, 10, 11, 12, 14, 19 and 21 — brown.
- Pieces 4 and 7, and nose — pink.
- Piece 9 — light brown.
- Piece 16 — grey (or suitable colour for branch).
- Eyes, claws and whiskers — black

Sewing order

1 1 + 2
2 (1,2) + 3
3 4 + 5
4 7 + 8
5 (4,5) + 6 + (7,8)
6 9 + 10
7 11 + 12
8 (9,10) + (11,12)
9 (4-8) + (9-12)
10 13 + 14
11 (13,14) + 15
12 (1-3) + (4-12) + (13-15)
13 18 + 19 + 20
14 21 + 22
15 17 + (18-20) + (21,22) + 23
16 (1-15) + 16 + (17-23)
17 Applique or embroider the nose, eyes, and claws, and embroider the lines for the whiskers.

Possum

1 square = 1 cm (⅜″)

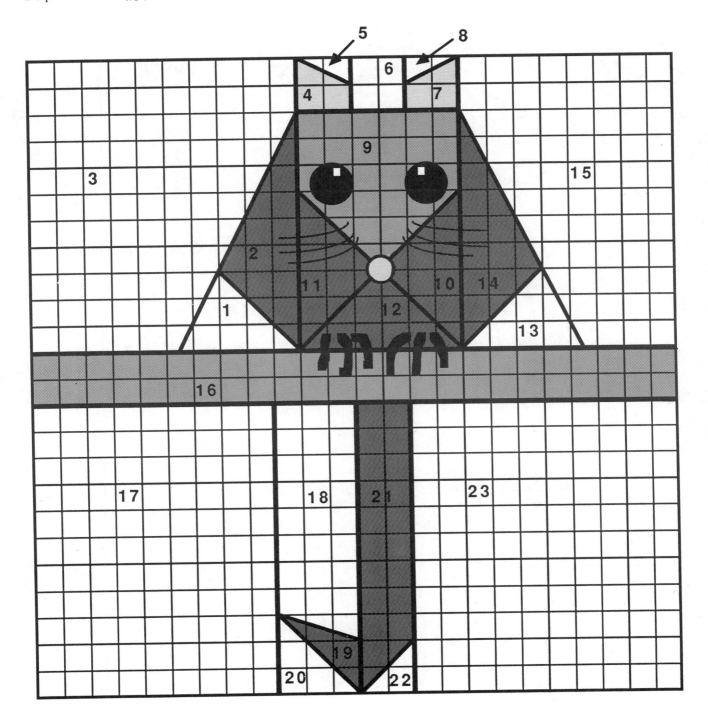

Emu

The Emu is a very large flightless bird common throughout the grasslands of Australia. The hen lays the eggs, which the male then incubates.

Colours

- Piece 1 — light brown or grey.
- Pieces 2, 3, 5, 6, 7, 9, 10, 13 and 16 — background.
- Pieces 4 and 8 — brown.
- Piece 11, 12, 14 and 15 —yellow.
- Eye — black.

Sewing order

1 1 + 2
2 (1,2) + 3
3 (1-3) + 4
4 (1-4) + 5
5 (1-5) + 6
6 7 + 8
7 (1-6) + (7,8)
8 (1-8) + 9
9 12 + 13
10 15 + 16
11 10 + 11 + (12,13) + 14 + (15,16)
12 (1-9) + (10-16)
13 Applique or embroider the eye.

Emu

1 square = 1 cm (⅜")

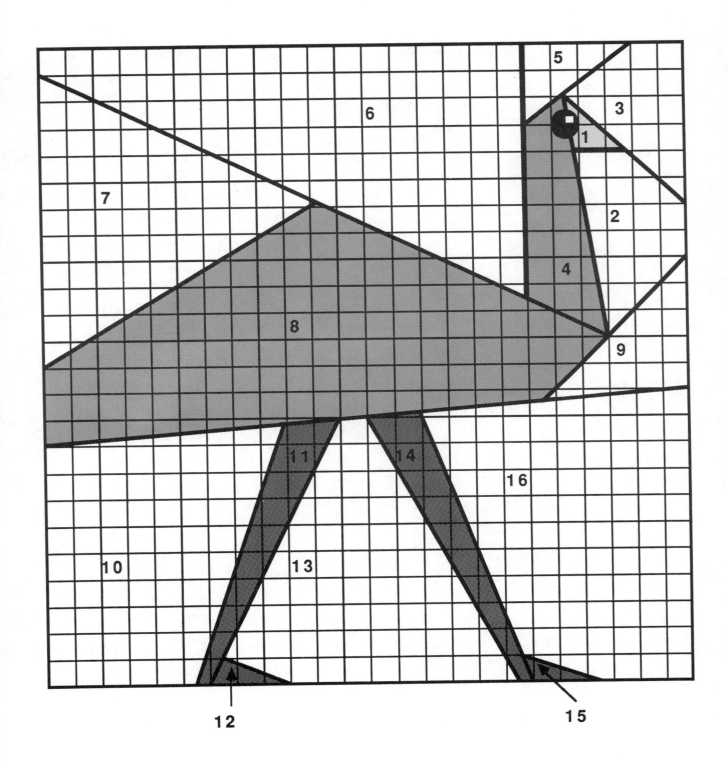

Kookaburra

Kookaburras are large kingfishers, although they mostly eat lizards, snakes and insects. They have a loud cry that sounds like raucous laughter.

Colours

- Pieces 1, 3, 4, 9, 12, 13, 17 and 19 — background.
- Pieces 2, 6, 8, 11, 15 and 18 — bone.
- Pieces 5 and 14 — dark grey or brown.
- Pieces 7 and 16 — brown.
- Piece 21 — rust.
- Piece 10 — cream.
- Pieces 20 and 22 — light grey (or suitable colour for a log).
- Eye — black.

Sewing order

1 1 + 2 + 3
2 4 + 5 + 6 + 7 + 8
3 9 + 10 + 11
4 (1-3) + (4-8) + (9-11)
5 (1-11) + 12
6 13 + 14
7 15 + 16 + 17
8 (15-17) + 18
9 (13,14) + (15-18)
10 (13-18) + 19
11 20 + 21 + 22
12 (1-12) + (13-19) + (20-22)
13 Applique or embroider the eye.

Kookaburra

1 square = 1 cm (⅜″)

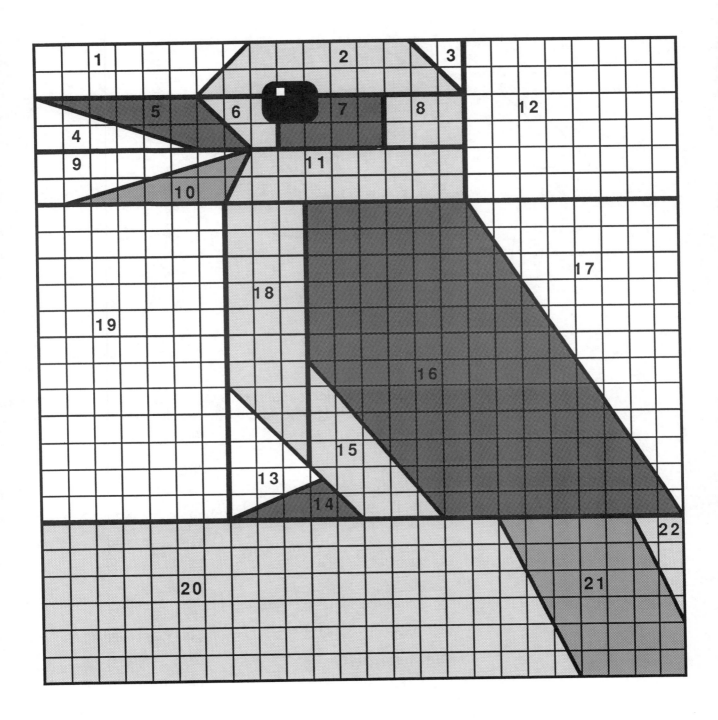

Kangaroo

PAR

Kangaroos are large marsupials which use their strong back legs to bound along. They are very common throughout country Australia.

Colours

- Pieces 1, 3, 5, 8, 9, 10, 12, 13, 16, 17, 19, 21 and 23 — background.
- Pieces 2, 4, 6, 7, 11, 14, 15, 18, 20 and 22 — brown.
- Piece 24 — light brown (or suitable colour for ground).
- Eye and nose — black.

Sewing order

1 1 + 2 + 3

2 4 + 5

3 (4,5) + 6

4 (1-3) + (4-6)

5 7 + 8

6 (7,8) + 9

7 (1-6) + (7-9)

8 10 + 11 + 12

9 13 + 14

10 (13,14) + 15

11 (13-15) + 16

12 17 + 18 + 19

13 20 + 21

14 (20,21) + 22

15 (17-19) + (20-22)

16 (13-16) + (17-22)

17 (10-12) + (13-22)

18 (1-9) + (10-22)

19 (1-22) + 23 + 24

20 Applique or embroider the nose and eye.

Kangaroo

1 square = 1 cm (⅜″)

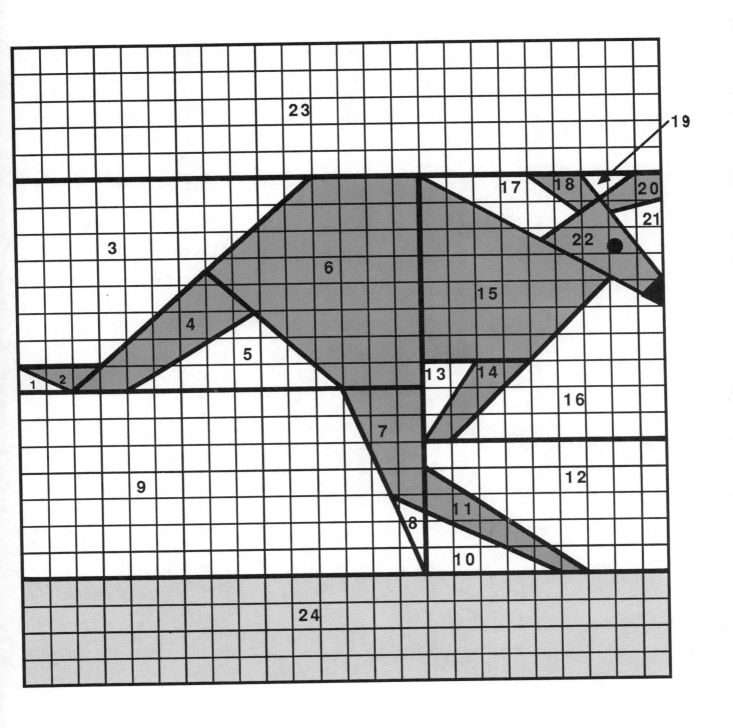

Sulphur-crested cockatoo (I)

PAR

Colours

- Pieces 1, 3, 5, 7, 9, 11, 13, 15, 17 and 18 — background.
- Pieces 2 and 19 — black.
- Pieces 4, 6, 8, 10 and 12 — yellow.
- Pieces 14 and 16 — white.
- Piece 20 — brown (or suitable colour for a log).

Sewing order

1	1 + 2
2	(1,2) + 3
3	5 + 6
4	7 + 8
5	9 + 10
6	11 + 12
7	4 + (5,6) + (7,8) + (9,10) + (11,12) + 13
8	14 + 15
9	16 + 17
10	18 + 19 + 20
11	(4-13) + (14,15) + (16,17) + (18-20)
12	(1-3) + (4-20)
13	Applique or embroider the eye.

The Sulphur-crested cockatoo is found in eastern and northern Australia. It has a discordant screeching cry, and often large flocks are seen in country areas.

Sulphur-crested cockatoo (l)

1 square = 1 cm (⅜″)

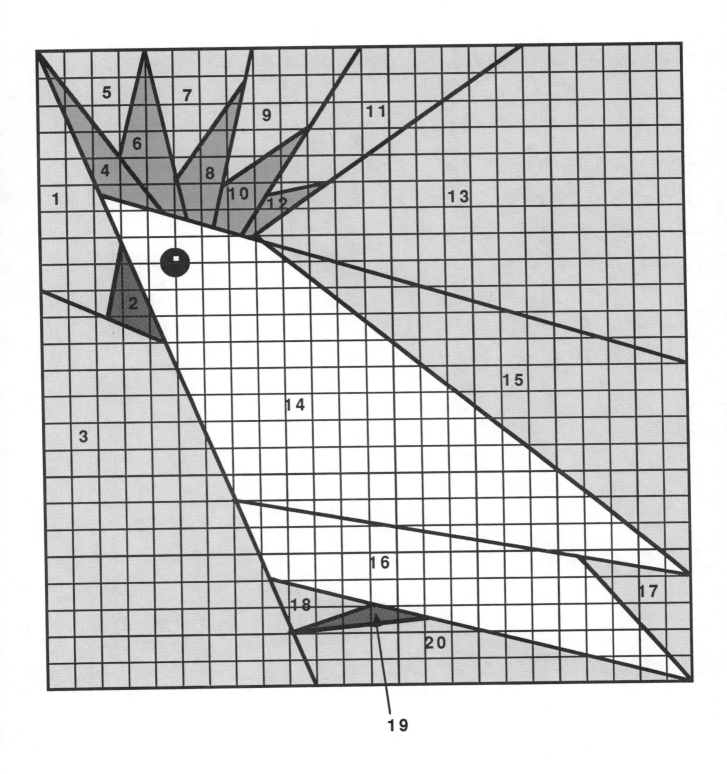

Sulphur-crested cockatoo (II)

Colours

- Pieces 1, 3, 5, 7, 9, 11, 13, 15, 17, 18, 19, 21, 22 and 26 — background.
- Piece 2 — grey or black.
- Pieces 4, 16, 20, 23 and 25 — white.
- Pieces 6, 8, 10, 12, 14 and 24 — yellow.
- Eye — black.

Sewing order

1   1 + 2

2   3 + 4

3   (1,2) + (3,4) + 5

4   7 + 8

5   9 + 10

6   11 + 12

7   13 + 14

8   6 + (7,8) + (9,10) + (11,12) + (13,14) + 15

9   16 + 17 + 18

10   19 + 20 + 21

11   (16-18) + (19-21)

12   (6-15) + (16-21)

13   (1-5) + (6-21)

14   22 + 23 + 24 + 25 + 26

15   (1-21) + (22-26)

16   Applique or embroider the eye.

Sulphur-crested cockatoo (II)

1 square = 1 cm (⅜″)

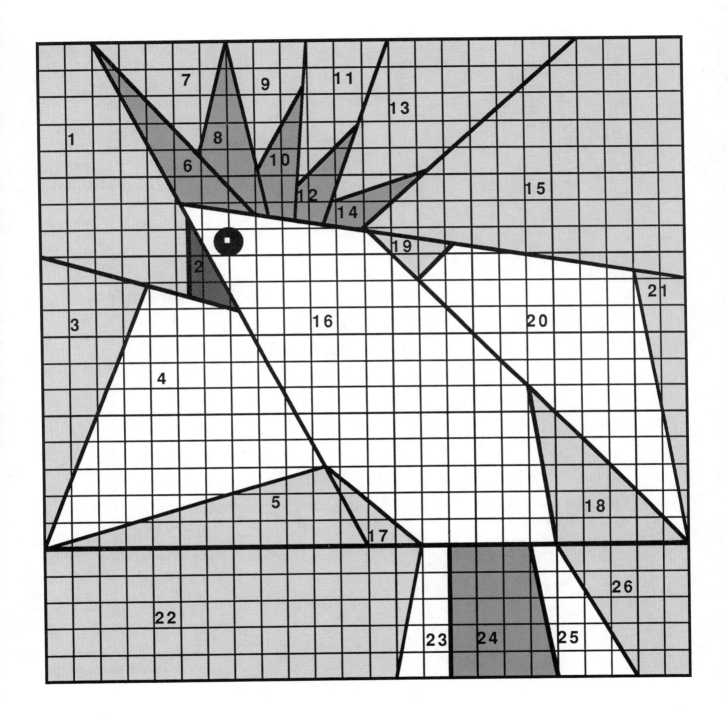

Frilled lizard

The Frilled lizard spreads out a large neck membrane and hisses when it feels threatened. This lizard is found in northern Australia.

Colours

- Pieces 1, 5, 6, 12, 13, 14, 19, 23, 26, 29 and 31 — background.
- Pieces 2, 11, 15 and 21 — light brown.
- Pieces 3, 7, 10, 17, 18, 20, 24, 25, 27, 28 and 30, and throat — brown.
- Pieces 4, 8, 9, 16 and 22 — cream.
- Eyes — black.

Sewing order

1   1 + 2 + 3 + 4 + 5
2   6 + 7 + 8
3   9 + 10 + 11 + 12 + 13
4   (1-5) + (6-8) + (9-13)
5   14 + 15 + 16 + 17
6   18 + 19
7   20 + 21 + 22
8   (18,19) + (20-22)
9   (14-17) + (18-22)
10   23 + 24
11   25 + 26 + 27
12   28 + 29 + 30 + 31
13   (23,24) + (25-27) + (28-31)
14   (1-13) + (14-22) + (23-31)
15   Applique or embroider the eyes and throat.

Frilled lizard

1 square = 1 cm (⅜″)

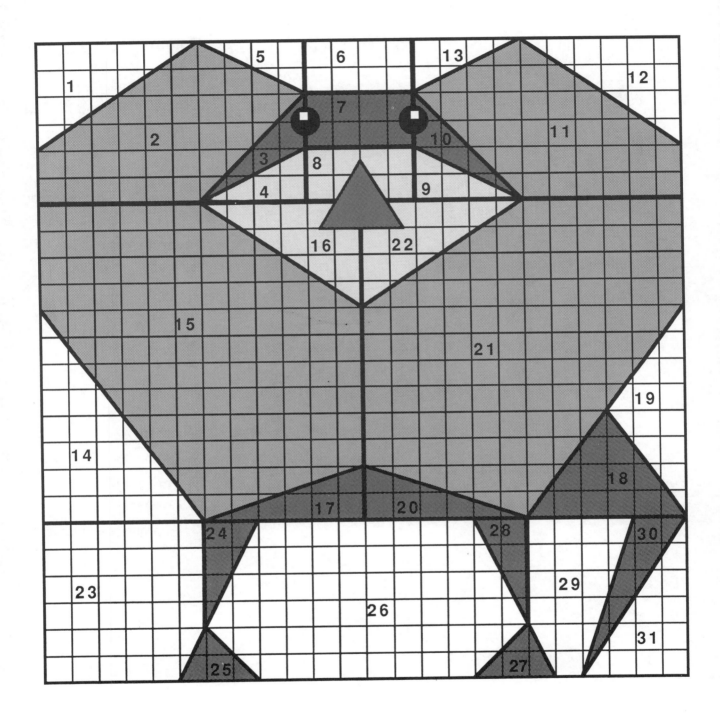

Pelican

PAR

The Australian pelican is similar to other pelicans throughout the world. Large and ungainly on land, it is stately and graceful in the air and on water.

Colours

- Pieces 1, 3, 7, 8, 11 and 13 — background.
- Pieces 2, 6, 9 and 12 — white.
- Pieces 4 and 5 and eye —black.
- Piece 10 — pink.
- Piece 14 — blue/green (or suitable colour for water).

Sewing order

1 1 + 2

2 3 + 4

3 5 + 6

4 (3,4) + (5,6)

5 (1,2) + (3-6) + 7

6 9 + 10

7 8 + (9,10) + 11

8 (8-11) + 12

9 (8-12) + 13

10 (1-7) + (8-13)

11 (1-13) + 14

12 Applique or embroider the eye.

Pelican

1 square = 1 cm (⅜″)

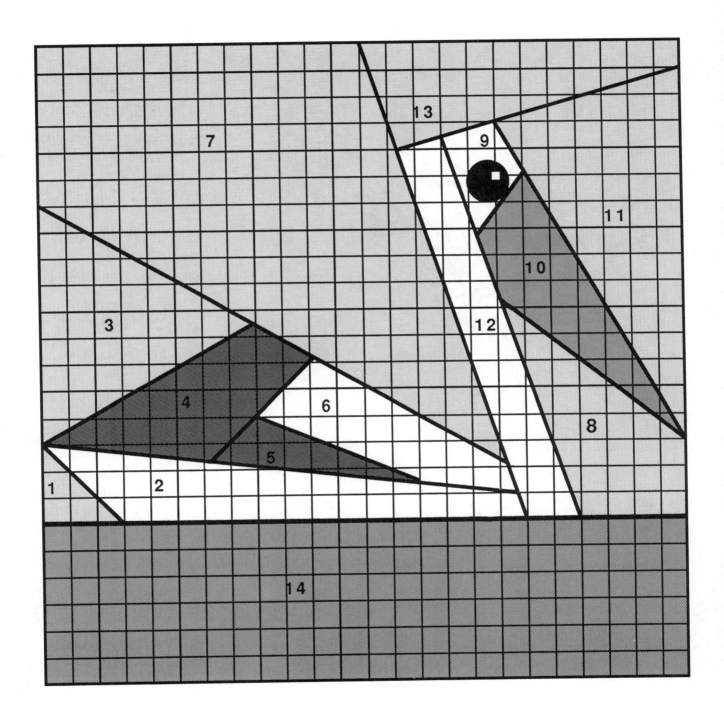

Blue wren

PAR

The Blue wren is one of many varieties of wren in Australia. It is a tiny jaunty bird, and is found throughout the south-east of the continent. The beautiful blue colouring of the male bird is seasonal.

Colours

- Pieces 1, 3, 6, 12, 13 and 14 — background.
- Pieces 2, 4, 7 and 9 — blue.
- Pieces 5 and 8, and eye and legs — black.
- Piece 10 — brown.
- Piece 11 — bone.

Sewing order

1 1 + 2 + 3

2 4 + 5

3 (4,5) + 6

4 (1-3) + (4-6)

5 7 + 8 + 9

6 10 + 11 + 12

7 (7-9) + (10-12)

8 (7-12) + 13

9 (7-13) + 14

10 (1-6) + (7-14)

11 Applique or embroider the eye, and embroider the legs.

Blue wren

1 square = 1 cm (⅜")

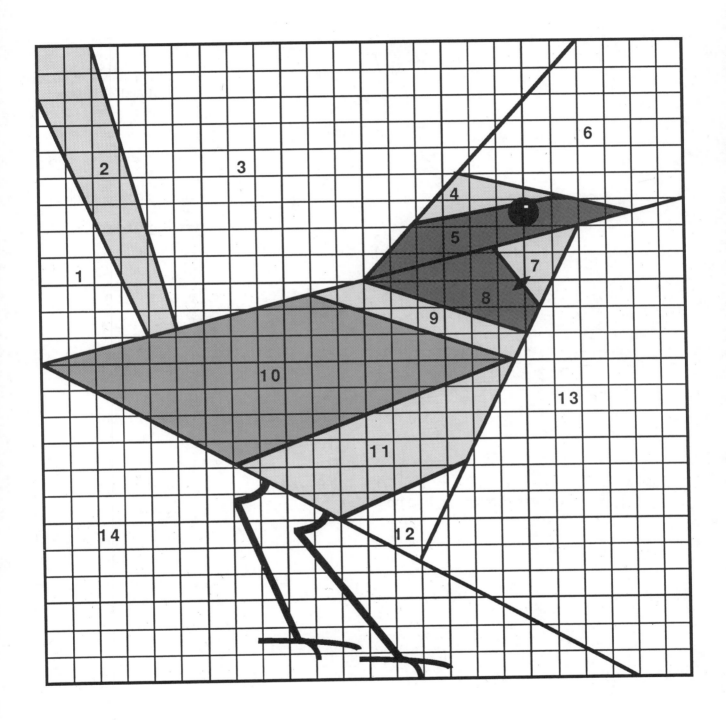

Wallaby

Wallabies are a species of small kangaroo. They are marsupials, so carry their young in a pouch.

Colours

- Pieces 1, 3, 5, 7, 9, 10, 12, 14, 17, 21 and 24 — brown.
- 2, 4, 6, 8, 11, 13, 15, 19, 20, 22 and 23 — background.
- Pieces 16 and 18 — light brown.
- Eye and nose — black.

Sewing order

1   1 + 2 + 3
2   4 + 5
3   6 + 7 + 8 + 9
4   (1-3) + (4,5) + (6-9)
5   11 + 12
6   10 + (11,12) + 13
7   14 + 15
8   (10-13) + (14,15)
9   16 + 17 + 18 + 19
10   20 + 21 + 22
11   (16-19) + (20-22)
12   23 + 24
13   (10-15) + (16-22) + (23,24)
14   (1-9) + (10-24)
15   Applique the eye and nose.

Wallaby

1 square = 1 cm (⅜″)

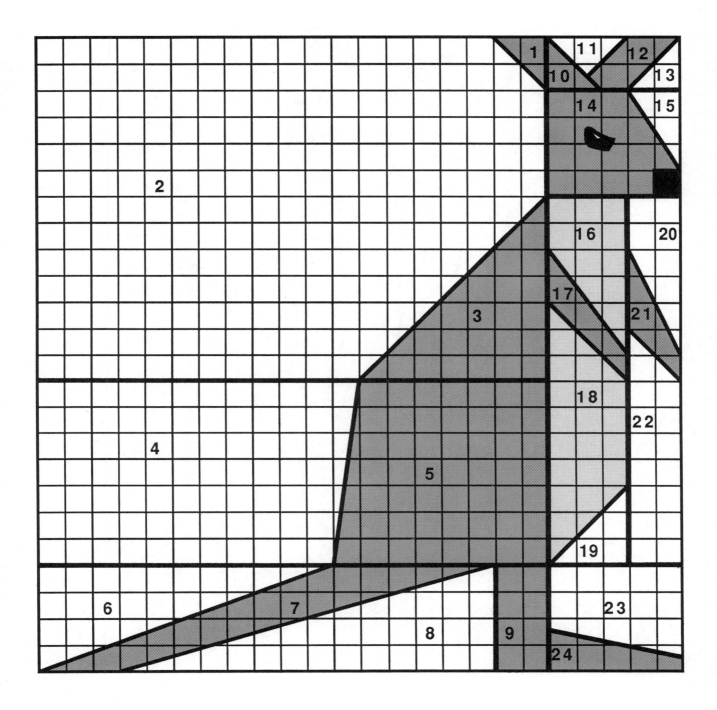

Gang-gang cockatoo

PAR

Gang-gang cockatoos live in the forests of south-eastern Australia. They feed on the seeds of trees, cracking the seeds with their strong bills, and are often seen in mated pairs.

Colours

- Pieces 1, 3, 5, 7, 8, 12, 14 and 16 — background.
- Piece 2 and claws — light brown.
- Pieces 4, 11 and 15 — grey.
- Pieces 6 and 13 — brown (or suitable colour for a branch).
- Pieces 9 and 10 — scarlet.
- Eye — black.

Sewing order

1 1 + 2
2 3 + 4
3 5 + 6 + 7
4 (1,2) + (3,4) + (5-7)
5 8 + 9
6 10 + 11
7 12 + 13 + 14
8 (12-14) + 15
9 (8,9) + (10,11) + (12-15)
10 (1-7) + (8-15) + 16
11 Applique or embroider the eye and claw.

Gang-gang cockatoo

1 square = 1 cm (⅜″)

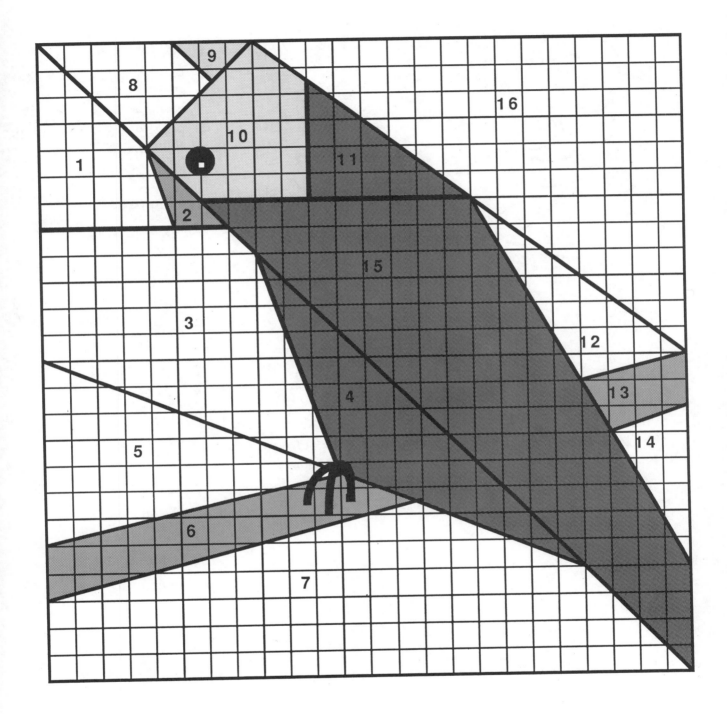

Green tree frog

The Green tree frog is just one of the many varieties of frog in Australia. It is a very large frog, and lives in trees in moist areas of north and eastern Australia.

Colours

- Pieces 1, 4, 6, 9, 10, 13, 14, 16, 17, 20, 21, 23 and 24 — background.

- Pieces 2, 3, 5, 7, 8, 11, 12, 15, 18, 19 and 22 — green.

- Eyes — black.

Sewing order

1   1 + 2

2   (1,2) + 3 + 4

3   6 + 7

4   (6,7) + 8 + 9

5   (1-4) + 5 + (6-9)

6   10 + 11

7   (10,11) + 12 + 13

8   14 + 15 + 16

9   (1-9) + (10-13) + (14-16)

10   17 + 18

11   (17,18) + 19 + 20

12   21 + 22 + 23

13   (17-20) + (21-23)

14   (17-23) + 24

15   (1-16) + (17-24)

16   Applique the eyes.

Green tree frog

1 square = 1 cm (⅜″)

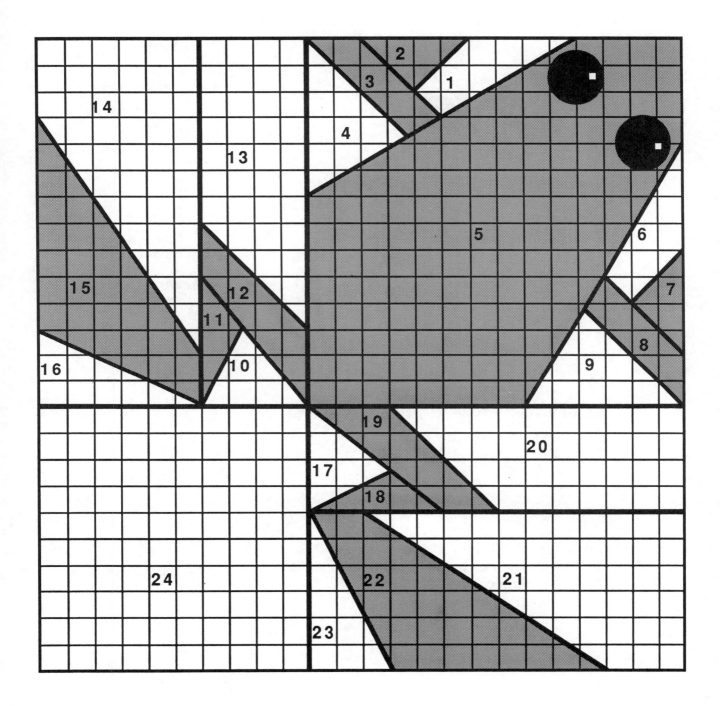

Boobook owl

The Boobook owl, also called the Mopoke because of the sound of its cry, eats beetles, moths and small mammals, and is found throughout Australia.

Colours

- Pieces 1, 6, 9, 10, 11, 15, 16 and 19 — background.
- Pieces 2, 5 and 7 — dark brown.
- Pieces 3, 4, 8, 13 and 14 — light brown.
- Piece 12 — brown.
- Pieces 17 and 18 — light tan.
- Eyes — yellow with black centres.

Sewing order

1 1 + 2 + 3
2 4 + 5
3 6 + 7 + 8
4 (1-3) + (4,5) + (6-8)
5 (1-8) + 9
6 11 + 12 + 13
7 14 + 15
8 18 + 19
9 16 + 17 + (18,19)
10 10 + (11-13) + (14,15) + (16-19
11 (1-9) + (10-19)
12 Applique or embroider the eyes and claws.

Boobook owl

1 square = 1 cm (³⁄₈″)

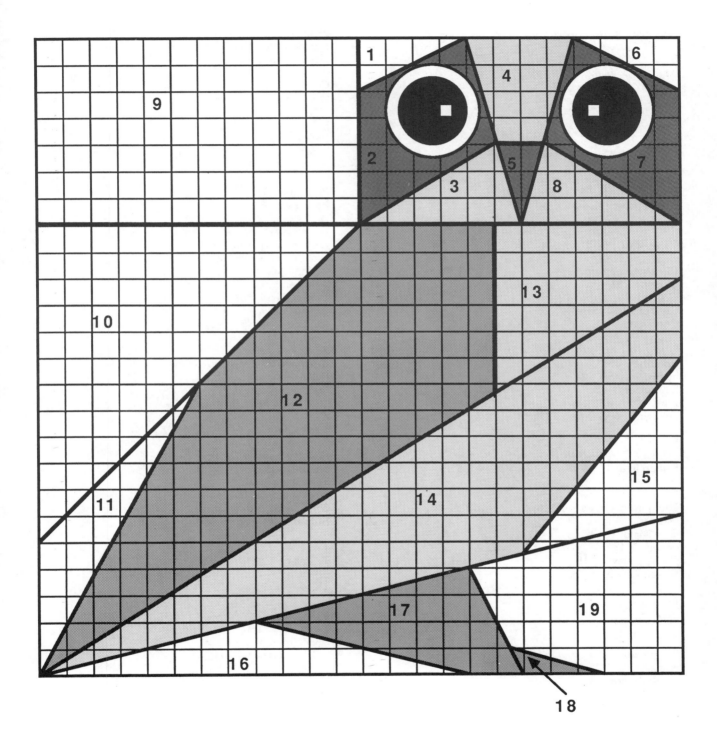

Index